PUFFIN BOOKS

THE LITTLE PUFFIN
BOOK OF MAGIC TRICKS

This tiny little book is
PACKED FULL
of tricks, jokes and puzzles!

Try
your fami
– they'
impre
your skills!

D1323214

PUFFIN BOOKS

UK | USA | Canada | Ireland | Australia
India | New Zealand | South Africa

Puffin Books is part of the Penguin Random House group of companies
whose addresses can be found at global.penguinrandomhouse.com.

puffinbooks.com

Penguin
Random House
UK

First published 2015
001

Copyright © Penguin Books Ltd, 2015

Text design by Mandy Norman
Printed in Great Britain by Clays Ltd, St Ives plc

A CIP catalogue record for this book is available from the British Library

ISBN: 978-0-141-36536-7

www.greenpenguin.co.uk

MIX
Paper from
responsible sources
FSC
www.fsc.org   FSC® C018179

Penguin Random House is committed to a
sustainable future for our business, our readers
and our planet. This book is made from Forest
Stewardship Council® certified paper.

THE LITTLE
PUFFIN
BOOK OF
MAGIC TRICKS

PUFFIN

Flick the book and see me move!

CONTENTS

Tricks
and
Illusions

The more you practise these tricks,
the more professional you will become!

MAGIC
Numbers

A simple *trick* to *amaze* your friends!

STEP 1:

Ask a friend to think of a number between **1** and **10**.

STEP 2:

Then **add** the **next higher** number to it.

STEP 3:

Add **9** and divide by **2**, and then **subtract the original number**.

STEP 4:

Pretend you can read their mind — the answer will always be **5**!

Here's another one:

4

STEP 1:

Ask a friend to think of a number **under 10** and **multiply it by 2**.

STEP 2:

Add **6** and **divide** the total by **2**.

STEP 3:

Then **subtract the original number**.

STEP 4:

Pretend you can read their mind — the answer will always be **3**!

TA-DA!

OPTICAL
Illusions

Trick your
brain into seeing
things that
aren't there!

HOW MANY COINS?

STEP 1:

Hold **two** ten-pence pieces between your index fingers.

STEP 2:

Rub the coins **up** and **down quickly** and watch what happens.

STEP 3:

It looks like a **third coin** magically appears from nowhere!

Is this a **candlestick?** Or is it **two faces in profile**?

Can you see both?

Is this a book pointing **towards** you, or **away**?

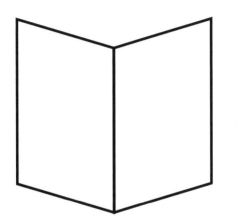

How many
shelves
are there?
Three or
four?

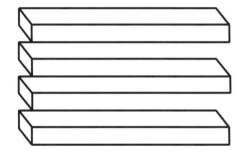

Look at the

two centre dots.

Is one bigger than

the other?

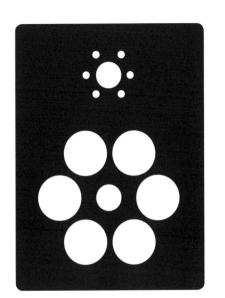

MAGIC
Rope Trick

You will need:
A long, thick piece of string

Secret preparation:
Tie a knot in one end of the string.

The trick:

STEP 1:

With **one end** of the string in **each hand**, show the audience that there are no knots.

Make sure you keep the knotted end hidden.

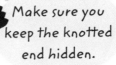

STEP 2:

Bring
**both ends
together**
and move your
hands as if you're
trying to knot it.

STEP 3:

Quickly drop
the end with
the knot and,
hey presto,
you have
magically tied
a knot in
the string!

Disappearing CUP

You will need:

A tea towel

A plastic cup

A coin

Preparation:

Sit at a table with your audience standing on the opposite side.

The trick:

STEP 1:

Put the coin on the table, **cover** it with the cup and place the **tea towel on top**.

STEP 2:

Lift up the **cup** and **tea towel together** and ask your audience to keep their eyes firmly on the coin.

STEP 3:

Discreetly drop the cup into your lap but continue to hold the tea towel as if the cup is still there.

STEP 4:

Quickly replace the **tea towel over the coin** and smash your hand down on it, as if pushing the cup through the table, and at the same time **drop the cup** from your lap on to the floor.

25

STEP 5:

Lift the tea towel to show that the coin is still there but the cup has fallen through the table.

WOW!

You will need:

A white plastic cup

A piece of sponge
(it should be bigger than the base of the cup)

A few ice cubes

Secret preparation:

Squash the sponge into

the bottom of the cup, then

add a few ice cubes.

28

The trick:

STEP 1:

Pour a small amount of water (about a centimetre) into the cup. The sponge will absorb the water.

STEP 2:

Blow into the cup, wave your hands over it and say the magic words.

STEP 3:

Turn over the cup and, *hey presto*, tip out the ice cubes!

Invisible
WRITING

30

You will need:

White paper

**White wax crayon
or a white candle**

White crayon

Water

Watercolour paint
– any colour will do

Paintbrush

The trick:

STEP 1:

Write your **secret message** on the paper using the white crayon or candle.

STEP 2:

To make the message appear, mix a little paint with water and brush over your paper.

Abracadabra!

Your secret message will appear!

There's nuffin' like a Puffin

Mirror
WRITING

Bamboozle your friends
with a **backwards message** –
they may need a **mirror** to read it!

I am a magician.

I like to perform
magic tricks.

Look out, or I may
saw you in half!

You will need:

A large bowl   Vinegar   Bicarbonate of soda   Food colouring

THE TRICK:

Pour 100ml vinegar into a bowl and **stir** in 3 teaspoons of bicarbonate of soda and a few drops of food colouring.

Watch the potion bubble and fizz — but make sure you DON'T DRINK IT!

MAGIC
COIN
TRICK

You will need:

A ten-pence piece

A long-sleeved shirt

SECRET PREPARATION:

Wearing your long-sleeved shirt, hold **one arm upright**, bent at the elbow, palm facing outward, and hand up level with your face as if you are waving.

Hello!

Put the coin in your sleeve, so that it sits just at your elbow. The long-sleeved shirt should hold it in place.

Practise dropping your arm down so that the coin slides out of your sleeve into your hand.

Now turn over for the actual trick!

The trick:

STEP 1:

Hold up your empty hand
so that the coin stays in place in
your sleeve and tell your audience
that you will now make a coin
magically appear.

STEP 2:

Show the audience
you have absolutely
nothing hidden in
either of your
hands.

Wave your other hand around
to distract your audience, and at the
same time drop your arm down
so that the coin slips out of
your sleeve and into
your palm.

STEP 4:

**Quickly bring
your palm back
up** and show everyone
how a coin has
magically appeared
in your hand.

*I'm
rich!*

LOOK,
no hands!

44

You will need:

A table

A straw

STEP 1:

Put the straw on the table and gently wriggle your fingers over it.

STEP 2:

Announce that you can make the straw roll by using your mind.

STEP 3:

Tell the audience to concentrate hard on the straw.

STEP 4:

Keep moving your hands, and at the same time **secretly blow** on the straw.

Everyone is
concentrating so hard
on the straw that they
won't notice you are
blowing it along
the table.

MAGIC POWERS

You will need:

A foil pie-dish   5 toothpicks   Washing-up
liquid

Secret preparation:

STEP 1:

Fill the foil pie-dish with just enough water to cover the bottom.

STEP 2:

Arrange four toothpicks in a **square shape** in the middle of the foil dish, making sure they **overlap** so that they stay together.

STEP 3:

Dip the fifth toothpick in the **washing-up liquid**.

The trick:

Gather your audience
around and tell them that you can
make the square of toothpicks
separate using your magic powers.

50

Take out your **toothpick
dipped in washing-up
liquid,** wave it above the dish,
then put the liquid-dipped end
into the middle of the square and
watch the toothpicks move apart!

It is the detergent in the washing-up liquid that causes this to happen.

51

Guess
the
Colour

You will need:

A small box of
wax crayons

The trick:

STEP 1:

**Facing away from the
audience**, hold the box of
wax crayons behind your back.
Without turning round, ask
someone to take the box of
crayons and put **one crayon
back in your hands**.

STEP 2:

With your hands still **behind your back**, turn round to face the audience. Then **scrape off** a little bit of the wax crayon using your **thumbnail.**

STEP 3:

Keep holding the crayon in one hand behind your back and wave the other in front as if reading the person's mind, taking a **quick look at your thumbnail** as you do so.

STEP 4:

Pretend to concentrate and then announce the colour of the crayon.

STEP 5:

Reveal the crayon to show you are right!

MAGIC CARD TRICK

You will need:

A pack of cards
(all face down)

Silently **count out twenty cards** off the top of the pack of cards and set them aside on a table in front of you. **This will be Pile 2.** The rest of the cards will be **Pile 1**.

The trick:

STEP 1:

Offer Pile 1 to your friend.
Ask them to choose a card,
memorize it and give it
back to you.

STEP 2:

Quickly slip the card beneath Pile 2 (the twenty cards you set aside at the beginning) and place Pile 2 on top of Pile 1.

STEP 3:

Turn the cards over to face you, so that you can see the front of each card. Count from the back of the pile until you get to the **twenty-first card**. That will be your friend's card.

STEP 4:

Ask,

'Is this your card?'

Hopefully it is!

MIND-BENDING

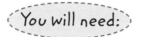

You will need:

A bent coin – ask a grown-up
to bend it carefully for you. Secretly
hold it in one hand before you
perform the trick.

The trick:

STEP 1:

Borrow a coin from someone
in the audience.

STEP 2:

Secretly swap it with the bent coin that you already have in your hand.

STEP 3:

Hold your hand over the audience member's and gently place the bent coin in their hand.

STEP 4:

Tell them you are going to **concentrate very hard** so that the coin starts to bend.

STEP 5:

When they open their hand they will see the **bent coin**. Tell them that you made it bend with your **powers of concentration**!

MAGIC

W O R D

S E A R C H

Find the **hidden** words!

MAGIC	**TRICKS**
SPELLS	**WITCH**
TREAT	**WIZARD**

The words can be found in all directions, including diagonally.

```
S U C D W U M S C U
T K R U F E L G L E
W S C X E L G A S Q
D I D I E M A G I C
R M T P R Y T H N V
A V S C M T R X Z Q
Z H Z M H G E F C T
I S F D W C A D I N
W R G T E C T Q O Z
M I L Z W B K S C N
```

Did you have fun
with the magic tricks?
Why not try out these
mischievous tricks on your
friends and family . . . ?

Magical
Mischief

Wiggly
Worm

Make a *worm-sized hole* in a peach with a toothpick by wiggling the toothpick around a bit.

Then poke in a **thin jelly-worm** sweet.

Give the peach to your friend and watch as they bite into it ...!

Aaaargh!

Yuck!

Before your next family dinner, **take the salt out** of the salt shaker and *replace it with sugar.*

Laugh as your family look surprised at their **funny-tasting food**!

My scrambled egg tastes of sweets. Yuck!

NEWS SHOES

Issue 1

HIDE some scrunched-up sheets of newspaper inside your family's shoes.

Watch your family struggle as they try to put their shoes on!

Sponge Cake

Take a new round bath-sponge, cover it with *icing and sprinkles* so it looks like a cake.

Leave it on the counter and see if your **family take a bite**!

While no one's watching, I think I'll have some of that!

76

Wrap a raisin inside a paper tissue.

Pretend you've just *swatted* a fly and pick it up with the tissue.

Then open it and **eat the fly** in front of your disgusted friend!

SUPER GROSS!

There's a
MOuse
in the
House

Put a **plastic mouse** in your mother's slippers and cover your ears as she *screams* the house down!

AAAAAH!

A Toothy Treat

Put some **cream-filled biscuits** on a plate.

Carefully separate the two halves and **scrape out the filling**.

Replace with white toothpaste and stick the biscuits back together.

Get ready to double up with laughter – and **run for your life** – when someone takes a bite!

Tv Trouble

Take the batteries out of your **TV remote** and giggle when no one's able to change channel!

I wanted to watch the news!

And I wanted to watch the *Best Ever Bake-Off!*

Poo!

Scatter *chocolate raisins* around the house and tell everyone they are **mouse droppings**.

85

Then pick one up, **pop it into your mouth** and watch the look of horror on everyone's face as you eat it!

86

A lychee is a small white fruit that looks rather like an eyeball but tastes delicious.

Gently *hollow out* a lychee with a small teaspoon to make an *olive-sized hole*.

Put an olive into the hole, then *poke a raisin* into the olive and *voila!*

An edible eye!

MAGIC
BOOK QUIZ

Can you guess the *titles* of these
magical children's books
from the clues?

Answers on page 118.

1

A boy with a **scar** on his forehead goes to *wizard school*.

2

A boy called _Bastian_ becomes involved in a quest to save _Fantastica._

3

A little girl
falls down a
rabbit hole.

4

A girl
called
Dorothy
just wants
to go
home.

5

A sand-fairy
is able to grant
wishes.

WIZARD

WORD

SEARCH

Find the hidden words!

CAPE	MAGICIAN
GLOVES	MIRROR
HAT	WAND

The words can be found in all directions, including diagonally.

I	Z	X	Q	G	N	K	X	G	D
N	H	L	E	S	Q	A	J	L	R
N	A	O	F	S	R	L	Q	I	D
F	T	I	Y	Q	G	A	M	W	R
R	B	N	C	D	F	U	K	H	V
R	O	R	R	I	M	C	D	L	M
S	E	V	O	L	G	W	C	B	X
L	S	R	J	S	M	A	Z	U	O
V	S	R	X	Y	P	N	M	Y	H
F	R	E	T	E	N	D	V	P	D

Answers on page 119.

Mixed-up
MAGICIANS

Answers on page 120.

These **famous magicians** have got themselves in a muddle.

Can you sort them out?

1 **OUHDINI**

CLUE: he was a famous escapologist

— — — — — — —

2 **DMYNAO**

CLUE: had his own TV show called *Magician Impossible*

— — — — — —

3 **ALUP NADEILS**

CLUE: had the longest-running TV magic show in the UK

— — — —

— — — — — — — —

4 **DVADI LIANEB**

CLUE: best known for his unusual stunts

— — — — —

— — — — — — —

5 STOOY

CLUE: although he doesn't speak, his famous catch phrase is 'Izzy wizzy let's get busy'

_ _ _ _ _

6 ERERND RWONB

CLUE: best known for reading people's minds

_ _ _ _ _ _

_ _ _ _ _

7 AIVDD FIELDCOPPER

CLUE: the illusionist who made the Statue of Liberty disappear!

— — — — — —

— — — — — — — — — —

Magic Show!

Add these jokes to your magic show
to warm up the crowd!

What does a **vampire** take for a bad cold?

Coffin drops.

102

What do you call a **magician** on a plane?

A flying sorcerer.

What do **ghosts** eat on Halloween?

Ghoulash!

What do **witches** put on their hair?

Scare spray!

What do **witches** put on their bagels?

Scream cheese!

What is a **magician's** best subject in school?

Spelling!

What do witches ask for at hotels?

Broom service!

Which **monster** plays
tricks on Halloween?

Prank-enstein!

What's the problem with **twin witches**?

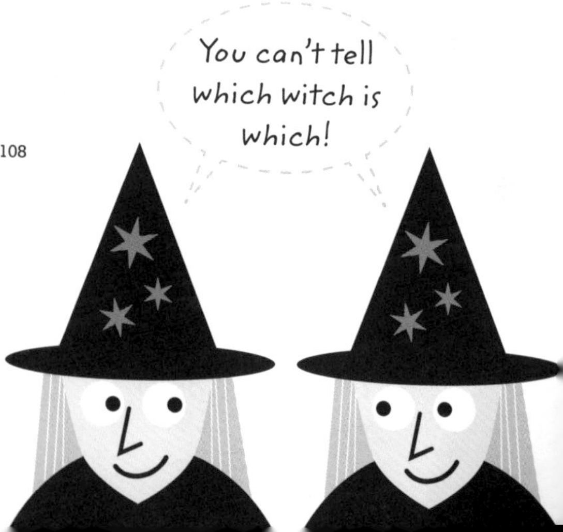

The *magician* got so mad he pulled his *hare* out.

'What's your **father's occupation**?' asked the teacher on the first day of school.

110

'He's a **magician**,' said the new boy.

'How interesting. What's his **best trick**?'

'He **saws** people in **half.**'

'**Gosh!** And do you have any brothers or sisters?'

'Yes, one half-brother and two half-sisters!'

Why do **wizards** brush their teeth three times a day?

To stop bat breath.

Why didn't the **skeleton** dance at the Halloween party?

Because he had no body to go with.

113

Who was the most famous skeleton **detective**?

Sherlock Bones.

What did the doctor say to the witch in hospital?

With any luck you'll soon be well enough to get up for a **spell**!

115

If a **wizard** was knocked out by **Dracula** in a fight, what would he be?

Out for the count.

MONSTROUS

WORD SEARCH

Find the **hidden** words!

BAT	**GHOUL**
HALLOWEEN	**MONSTER**
GHOST	**VAMPIRE**

*The words can be found in all directions,
including diagonally.*

R	L	T	D	B	T	F	E	T	M
H	E	A	X	S	A	O	R	N	V
K	F	T	O	M	V	T	I	W	V
O	B	H	S	K	H	R	P	P	E
A	G	O	U	N	B	E	M	Y	L
G	H	O	U	L	O	T	A	G	N
Q	Y	T	H	E	Y	M	V	F	L
U	I	Q	Y	L	A	P	X	Y	P
N	E	E	W	O	L	L	A	H	C
Y	P	S	R	Q	N	Z	E	S	V

Answers on page 119.

Answers

MAGIC
BOOK QUIZ

Pages 88–93

1. *Harry Potter and the Philosopher's Stone*
2. *The Neverending Story*
3. *Alice's Adventures in Wonderland*
4. *The Wizard of Oz*
5. *Five Children and It*

Page 65:
Magic Word Search

S	U	C	D	W	U	M	S	C	U
T	K	R	U	F	E	L	G	L	E
W	S	C	X	E	L	G	A	S	Q
D	I	D	I	E	M	A	G	I	C
R	M	T	P	R	Y	T	H	N	V
A	V	S	C	M	T	R	X	Z	Q
Z	H	Z	M	H	G	E	F	C	T
I	S	F	D	W	C	A	D	I	N
W	R	G	T	E	C	T	Q	O	Z
M	I	L	Z	W	B	K	S	C	N

Page 95:
Wizard Word Search

I	Z	X	Q	G	N	K	X	G	D
N	H	L	E	S	Q	A	J	L	R
N	A	O	F	S	R	L	Q	I	D
F	T	I	Y	Q	G	A	M	W	R
R	B	N	C	D	F	U	K	H	V
R	O	R	R	I	M	C	D	L	M
S	E	V	O	L	G	W	C	B	X
L	S	R	J	S	M	A	Z	U	O
V	S	R	X	Y	P	N	M	Y	H
F	R	E	T	E	N	D	V	P	D

119

Page 117:
Monstrous Word Search

R	L	T	D	B	T	F	E	T	M
H	E	A	X	S	A	O	R	N	V
K	F	T	O	M	V	T	I	W	V
O	B	H	S	K	H	R	P	P	E
A	G	O	U	N	B	E	M	Y	L
G	H	O	U	L	O	T	A	G	N
Q	Y	T	H	E	Y	M	V	F	L
U	I	Q	Y	L	A	P	X	Y	P
N	E	E	W	O	L	L	A	H	C
Y	P	S	R	Q	N	Z	E	S	V

Pages 96–100

120

And that's what we call magic!

It all started with a Scarecrow . . .

Puffin is over **70** years old.

Sounds ancient, doesn't it?
But Puffin has never been so lively.

From the very first Puffin story book
about a man with broomstick arms called
Worzel Gummidge to **Matilda** and
Artemis Fowl, today there's a Puffin for
everyone. Whether it's a picture book or
a paperback, a sticker book or a joke book,
if it's got that little Puffin on it –
it's bound to be good.

READ, WRITE, LISTEN, BLOG, DREAM, WIN . . .

Did you know that Puffin also records audiobooks and invents apps?

Find out more at
puffin.co.uk